RAY DI PALMA

RAIK

Fa presto zampogna della sgrignutuzza

ROOF

This book was made possible,
in part, by a grant from the New York State
Council on the Arts.

Design by Elizabeth DiPalma
Production by Susan Bee
Typeset by Strong Silent Type
Author photo by Olita Day

ISBN 0-937804-37-1
Library of Congress Catalog Card No.: 89-62801

ROOF BOOKS
are published by
The Segue Foundation
303 East 8th Street
New York, N.Y. 10009

RAIK

20 minutes of indolence
44 years of speculation
emblematic pretext five
flexes or more to tenor
the specific molded ilk

qua specifics qua welts
polygonal totem fissure
times the restored form
the shape qua shape had
had in mind for thought

tuned bricks and musics
hulled equinox glaciers
spooned tomes in replay
your own words stressed
with haste and progress

parabolas and pigmented
ratios ink added to ink
metonymy squat as a qua
renaming and disabusing
murks and economy of it

Put a loud vowel
in a clay shadow
hang your eye in

Egyptian fashion
stone piled itch
swells splinters

oversee the raft
advancing toward
the seven formed

You trick my owl
and change music
to hidden primes

Figure of else's
stake to conceal
prod for oar and

Length for hands
mirage waits for
the long vowel I

Place in the eye
testimony builds
for your secrecy

Share the warmth
threefold within
marks for breath

Thin gray oboed coves
reach the double word
astonished by the ode

real common and not a
lavish scheme excited
or proportioned by an

entablature like this
model meshed aires of
response and calls to

cull for human noises
teasing and pressings
hammer to wire string

to vibrating boards a
fretted sequence note
for tempered note has

thought shadow enough
rocklike or evergreen
tune's cricket metier

A neutral tether
paced from sound
to sound keeps a
lexical torque a
winding resolves
repairing chance
with certain aim
cast away secant
to secant tether
apex to apex X's

Taboo stake this
connection lyric
focus gathers on
the shared split
tightest packets
bound for knocks
and drifts torts
remembered along
an edge factored
to secant tether

Carbon dart bees
locate blood law
truth's paint in
the glove dreams

Song tasters are
asking for names
colorless window
in the spine box

Hardmouth pastel
writes grammar's
plug examples in
self-made colors

Welders' weather
readiness mirage
the scar a style
fit for limelite

Affective vapors
in the dust make
abstract marking
emphatic in lore

Lark carols numb
curves skep bark
bring likeness a
vacant sheen and

vouches formulae
wrong zone wrong
contradictions a
set of token Ohs

Coherence socket
bone roll timbre
styptic hymns or
trumpet cypher a

burdened solaced
anecdote lip and
tongue say spite
or hunted graces

Loosened tongues
put out the fire
turning the wick
ten turns to see

The generous terms
make an undertow I
plot with hilarity
and remorseless st

utter holding more
than passionate my
continuing failure
to find a set tide

beginning with all
names residual and
flown from moments
words could anchor

bulked with a sure
measure of tact or
the fatal sound of
lucidity's capture

mock rhythms start
and stop rehooking
the anvil to sleep
eros red as reason

zone one one one on zone one
no one zone one one zone one
one no zone zone one one one
zone one zone on one one one
zone one zone one on one one
zone on zone one one one one

architectures the buildup at
the foot of the unity put up
one zone on one zone one one
one zone one on one zone one
radial in forgotten fraction
one one of one zone one zone

out of one add one or another
techtonic cogs one into other
recognition logs the zone and
the one zone to one zone lift
extension codes in one to one
no quandary no codes just one

friction logs the code no one
to one or one on one can zone
nouns and under nouns zones a
figment the finale smoked-out
pursuit tattoo noun-coded cog
tooth set gear to zone on one

mine's the forged gloss
the light under the sun
paper soaked in tea pen
cut and blunt as a dome

enamel pearl and smokey
barm loose calculations
such and such to answer
such and such and calls

to answer calls fakhirs
to answer fakhir's call
faience art beards with
hornrim guise to modify

common boiled and local
sense sharp and complex
view's fray accrued and
the enigma's value cued

eidetic dollar coins in
basic clues a tautology
the swift's horizons my
site with circle's eyes

reason
figure
the to
the my
assays
signal
animal
noting
the to
the an
answer
asking
answer
choirs
of X=Y

stasis
a lark
sexual
allure
gauges
the to
the or
proper
sounds
linear
method
expels
etymon
to the
etymon

sulks in crisis
talks in motion
clouts grabbing
at random signs
and random term

to expedite and
render smooth a
systematic loud
and migrant sky
over my content

canticle orbits
plainsong night
after night and
a frost lingers
to rime with me

multiply by one
eluding distant
pace tangential
cunning measure
step to my step

saxophone riddle boom
agenda umbrella stave
and calendar gravures
set this gangster ode
limousine flesh and a
short black-skirt sky
send lawyers guns and
money halo rounds all
icon red as milk mist
in the theoried light

ambulance traffic and
subway seam moods cat
bone Euclid so favors
the phrase its din so
lamps the love man so
the noon wrist tables
this uncharted volume
aching on the eardrum
not spider whisper or
beam of repartee this

real aire real snarls
of primordial vapours
without scruple or an
inward soul to banter
with the outward pace

Fog mottle the deep board
Ironic screeches a matter
For the middle road north
Mud plank and bog harvest

Blue boot windmill divide
curved waters bark impact
buttons of coal the knees
tucked in the sullen bias

Blank turns and thin rags
Propose the shorn knocker
To argue the basket empty
Or full its horizon bread

Thick-voiced disgrace and
the hobbled mule coughing
in the snow mile piles on
mile where no road shines

Chinese song derived
from the swamp grass
bindings green golds
yellow on red meters

the eclectic drudges
pluck the heat black
fingers balance bird
votives with painted

pages of faded charm
stone drapes candles
in stuccoed catacomb
red hand to kohl eye

Broth blankets beards and beer
fish spears at the throat axis
spirals in the dialect's blood
fluent races of cutter-navvies
to set the sun temple straight
build roads and sing the idiom

Sacrifices at the river's edge
ratify sepulture codex brumous
rushlit options squared theses
pine-valanced moonyard transit
corrosive mandates and vigil's
clock iron pinions for tongues

Sleep's hard ear mauls the tag
dream's tendoned hazard wolf's
lair rattle glooms the comfort
measured in the wick a jittery
owl turns metaphysic the hound
braying rigmarole at the stars

Set upon set against the tongue
anathemata from noon's tyro his
towny accents muck and moil ham
threads for rope lithic rhythms
more hammer than fretting blade
mulish constraints replace form

The cracking mirror coughs gold
Roman torches and coins mortise
tongue to idea and heap oxen on
leaves rot in the legion's salt
and spilled wine for the ritual
of flight and abandoned history
fugitives enrolled to march the
routes they cobble straight cut
from an arc and wedged diamonds
mirrored moons mirrored shadows

sentimental suspicion
synthesis contraption
refuge of words stone
and light the reaches
of the concentrated a
page and stiff eye to
hand entropy rib fist
first structure paths
block value's surgery
my name in a notebook
a manufactured memory
valves and values are
pump pipes piston and
bulls-eye percentages

interpretive harmony
burns in your throat
like the fuse in zig
zag more to air than
air movement cuts to
left and right pares
and pairs of hitched
flame consume tangle
and fan the obliques
of patience the open
hand implodes author
and text disposed to
interpretive harmony
singular modes focus

Flywheel sonorities & every story
a ghost story trim suspicions set
against infinity notch verb notch
to surrogate structure the plough
reinvented feedback scans answers
anticipatory emblems frame lodges
mere suspensions without option's
intricate equipoise siren call of
miscellanea articulating a cocoon
orthodoxy integrates the polished
enthusiasm with failed levitation

an adjacent ether stretches
the monosyllable the serial
moon charts the stagings of
the grid tides and amends a
web of hybrid paradoxes hid
in the mimetic-friction man
who slaps an echo into bas-
relief and counts the stars

Prester John and
Song of the Idea
talon pap signal
rage song of the

idea Prester Joe
Psalms of Arrows
diluvian gravels
song of the idea

his machine grit
engine float and
song of the idea
martyr pip width

low sand flaring
skeptic wind the
song of the idea
seals the slides

Marco Polo sings
tune of the idea
for Prester Jake
the salty scribe

El Lobo line by line
and lie you see loco
El Lobo hoot piu piu
galantuomo mai molto
wool of the wolf for
pazzo canto cantorum
El Loco formato loco
Lupo El Lobo piu mai
photo pillow chateau
tropo loco tropo sai

from the middle of a
mouth to the hollows
of an ear the oval O
from the middle of a
tongue to the hollow
of an eye the oval O
Homer hawking cyclic
rips and traipses my
routes lotus without
carving bowie within

quoted crystal again
local wood for these
towers & vaudevilles
roots in quicksand &
nothing known abound
dum capitolium aptly
scandet no praise no
grace titter to roar
dum capitolium folks
scandet El Lobo rows

scelerous cursitors
abound scelerous to
dicker o'clock cony
huggering cursitors
buskill and scratch
patches jet & apple
squires traffic the
foin smokes the nip
all queer-ken lusks
scelerous cursitors
prig the high-pad &
for pedlars' French
who cuts whids bene
or queer unleaguers
& multa latent quae
non patent (stalled
to the rogue) Gerry
gan! dup the jigger
cut cant tour maund
Goneril's doggerels
or niggle and scour
cramp-rings on this
chats where canteth
tour ye a nase nabs
my issue to hiss me

one comes sharp to
the silence of the
origin or response
to the retreat and
sums of divergence

counted or colored
flagged with music
attentive to pause
drift is demograph
footprints conceal

divisions footfall
acoustics behind a
shadow detach what
lacks for intrigue
tango clues or the

yield momentum got
radiance erodes an
objective grabbing
the multiplied for
its anonymous tale

you can read about
the prisoner's eye
for sudden motives
pricked out around
the lapidary fault

sanctions no comment
efforts no comment a
sanction of comments
and efforts to amend
comments sanction an
amended comment when
sanctions amend when
no sanction commends
the amended sanction
no comment no amends
no efforts to amends
comment and sanction
amends amended amend
sanctions of comment
amends amendeds amen

shamble of weird argument speech
alone no music walls inhabitants
in masks monkeys scrambling acro
batic phobias and short lanes to
the dry stockades white scum and
sediment in marble basins acorns
and starlings cracked slate tile
and white iron mud lozenges mixt
with fragrant oils conduits to a
small sulphurous pool and canals
Wednesday Sept 27th 1581 arrived

I stretch the rudimentary
until it dreams the count
volunteered specifics and
brutal parlance analogues
and lapstrake proportions
imposed renditions hidden
in the summoned syllables
ancient cross sections of
ancient reference atom of
keener demand or rudiment

madrigals full of suspicions
mexican pencil tibetan paper
russian paper italian pencil
a mechanical porridge poured
out of torque and this steam
augur puts in turn and turns
out the twists of the summer
snakes' friezes in floodline
hoaxing of fertile clarities
wrapped in an idea following
an idea rondo marked allegr⊕
the small target focused the
final 'O' the agenda of some
missing page baroque as milk

song genders in silence
seed in a broken circle

a transient pulse lifts
the hand before a small

stalking caesura a moth
drums for drums shining

horns aslant the darker
constellations the grey

horse up to the stirrup
in lavender and orchard

bee mulberry leaves the
bluntworm   moonshalf

starshalf   spokehalf
fixedhalf   blackworm

whiteworm   seedshalf
seed in a broken circle

what is the status
of the quarry what
is the status of a
lair three decades
with three decades
to spare cardinals
ordinals for snare
what is the status
of the quarry what
is the status bare

the claims of myth and metaphor
the chanced measures & cadenced
mixtures a scheme of atmosphere
and a code of abstract quantity
or the decoded flux examined by
the periphery absorbed in these
lyrical takes on the axiomatick
instruments of eyebrow & threat
devious or unalloyed enthusiasm
turned commerce & trade's bland
refinements a susurrus of notes
diatribe smothered with dollars
hobbled allusions press the eye
there lurks Oedipus the Luddite

cargo between bait and delay
painted glass cigarettes and
dragonfly knives cut felt in
thick pads thick pads of tan
felt thick pads of rough cut
felt stacked and pressed cut
cargo between bait and delay
cut pressed and stacked felt
cut rough pads of thick felt
painted glass cigarettes and
dragonfly knives cut felt in
thick pads blunt tan pads of
cargo cut thick cargo baited
chained pads of thick felt a
dragonfly knife sharp enough
cut rough pads of thick felt
thick pads thick pads of red
felt rough cut thick pads of
cut felt stacked and pressed
dragonfly knife sharp enough

peripatetic in the status
quo convictions move like
the lizard a squander jot
beneath the tongue points
tact blunts tacks shadows
inside the painted rose a
terminus fox abides fox a
superstitious crocodile &
birdsong coincident makes
note for incident numbers
set upon numbers a grassy
enclosure where crouching
reptiles inspire some new
metamorphosis not a dream
but a bed in Ovid's poems
a plan a pattern monsters
that fly summer sentinels
coiled in the arbitrary &
eidetic energy hazard the
catalyst precipitates set
against ritual folding in
and out of myth an action
the atman extends through
form and the relinquished
mirrors numbers & tempers

spectral primer roaming the corner
of the ace's pole dead weight adds
to the wind miscut misblossom word
blind cool lodes swarm under thorn
hook buds poppystar the splintered
twitch and thick lurch speechraked
the blood dances in the nickflaked
tines crane beams through brambles
sheared reflexes straddled premon-
itions tin cool tracking screed as
sounds the ruts' rush sheds pearls
to fog spoor spur corona bolts ear
leaf and lung take the fold gabled
saurian hide rasp crooked in one's
beat a script of a second pavement
Pindar tuning Homer with a machine

in an ancient tongue ease was forfeit and
ill-will more readily comprehended when a
rank formalized esteem and a man's future
with petty ecclesiasts and jaded copyists
seeking stipends greed's optimists turned
"not now maybe later" threat & admonition

twice shared but crooked
in one beat formulations
on the run odd jars odds
and bangled fangs unions
scratches a stalk turned
summer limp in broadside
letters the taut thought
taught truths from Blake
angels whirrr and angels
were the handspin of and
this handspan of an idea
pennied contrition fills
the orient street vessel
with almond syllable and
cabled stone rime-scored
crescent and rime-scored
bolts recited the tilled
ravel twice beam-riddled
with angles and counts a
snap-quibbled digression
tantrum sketcht a circle

loud distractions the
worth's words charmed
stern or supersided &
intent on the stagger
short or grafted mood
my hurdy-gurdy Merlin
minister of sociality
fife after fife peaks
shrill and cordial an
island of reels above
and heed below stripe
and inlay more excess
secco sgrafitto loops
fancy's punctual mock

overandovergoes
formandform'sop
acityisislateri
sitlatertheveil
edinsideandoutt
oextendtherando
minthewaterstri
ppedofitspatina
rawradiantsurmi
seonelistenandt
wotransformlaug
hedandplacidpeg

a hammer's corrupted note
for note by the motion to
motive an agon corruption

dismantled fragment prods
fragment itinerant spokes
spondee's digit & taloned

dactyl recourse & methods
prelude subsequence gaffs
to widen the trifle shank

thridding prospects to my
wilier hues or colloquy's
thrall and blend of taunt

suited to error and hinge
squeal chopped logic gone
to an antick common gloss

symmetry's ornament dogs
the cleft familial stops
and yawns knots and lies
ascetic caution mechanic
and oracle orient the ox
in his order summa atque
pro bono's brought these
few to hold their breath
and consider the dust in
farming the platitude ah
ha yes I see yes what yr
up to with all this rime
to reason and I want too
to let you know I reckon
it stinks when personare
means resound I hear you

past surprise the past
surprises & improvised

tradition proto povera
flat bottom hewn rough

the peg's corner grabs
the hole's periphery &

marks for depth carved
balance and gauges the

width's curve embraces
of measure warped true

cedar thwarts & boiled
water fixing convexion

a neutral obstacle passes
into the sentences turned
toward insistent arranged

words voluptuously abrupt
a pagoda not a lighthouse
not behind or beneath the

haywire bulk of them when
tomorrow you accustom the
shadow to the universally

inconsequential despair's
formal guesswork and mine
a lighthouse not a pagoda

lazing through the rate of horizon
the vista supports the resolutions
open traps stack the gravity under
the trees binocular and bounded by
puzzles month to month puzzles and
some earnest vector vistas clashed
squint copse to ample invisibility
and so popped ardor continued this
reach blurring not strain nor hold
of a 13th moon ten trees and birds
primary risks to the idiom a tuner
unleashed tactic overreaches elegy
ambiguous permutation makes sparks
in the logos not statute and rigor
nominative alternity rare contexts

coarse harmonies more
tactile and proximity
out of issue the ends
of one staked to this
end of another risked
precedent cleated for
impression's measures

streaked leather mask
for age and resonance
departures begun in a
smokey hole penetrate
the illusion spectrum
and augmentative hive
allegro rest and pace

nude and interpretive
alibi the parts stuck
to the wind to define
pulse eroding current
twist a ledge of rain
and ice for certainty
anticipate my balance

prismatic up a dead end the parsing
congratulations probe the armatures
of the opportune earnest totems but
distinctions remain a mystery while
terror's stealth friend is mistaken
for patient ploy & background noise

the making infatuation
pursues departures not
direction irreversible

moods prove the genial
episode the unfinished
distances and diagrams

estimate and praise or
estimate and startle a
hawkyard chiming nouns

and asterisks hurrying
information expansions
on track to the common

colonies neon congress
and hark circumstances
filling out the strays

critics of faced space
Arkansas China bazaars
within the hard crease

quizzed elation island
to island or a robot's
whistle through a dark

opportunity the spoken
thumbscore or best day
to concentrate or best

day to foreground blue
flags generous to pure
coincidence about noon

a hardened sense of reality love
sleeps under a wooden mask faces
comprehension's fifth paraphrase

stray bullets interpret the dice
the curl of the pages splash ink
back into the word an anesthetic

source of revenue guides a droll
chorus punctuating some vigilant
purple joke the service rendered

etched on the pause creates that
unspecific inner silence uttered
and very tonic to the memory jaw

what was it French
riffling the palms

too long to find a
letter I two longs

to make a right is
it French riffling

the fronds in this
poem who to say of

its words thanks a
lot for the breeze

what is acknowledged
only what was wanted

authenticated vanity
the hardgraced spike

keyed night-yield of
sleep's hollow march

fracture and gabbled
dereliction textured

shrill as chalk dust
blown through a bone

marks mortal smother

an uprooted tree chained to a
Prometheus what is the status
of the quarry cool argent and
exposed pounding anxiety word
for word lucent nimbus quicks

bide to bide the by and by an
aim executed rites and cohort
tongue mulled into 'L's sharp
harvest challenged goaded and
shaped by the mutable tally a

qualm for the diadem or shoes
full of salt frank multitudes
taken in torpor deserted talk
skeins of mandate and prime's
zest the hottest wick affords

calcined necropolis vitus–up
your ballistic measure dodge
of influence and flattery to
earn a bit of sacking shroud
enfolding the malignant dust
disintegrating but indelible
like music the pulse brought
a chamade under Luxor's moon

more with than twined more aire
than more light to extol what's
owed the caked vault pit's loam

auriferous thickened fast to an
ochre runt culpable and numb or
thickened fast to the queried a

pendant rating full of the pink
stalled lumens of the assiduous
the skeptic's tattoo for legend

emptied of undoing by the twice
chewed bowl of reef nettle stew
mandarin panjandrum ornithopter

and passacaglia set their terms
kakemono or jussive thoughts in
the river hards white water cob

I salute the serial viand
sky coffee and briar wand
nudge up to the ampersand

the restless comprises an
interrupted invisible and
this pairs the parade and

your wit's end white hand
hooked to the bridge span
the darn stun knobs a man

barked wood snaps my faun
five good words ago stand
crammed shut in the bland

or spun into a rusted can
vortexing the crowd again
wheeling the clocked hand

jig's guile pled flat pent
to pencil a mention flexed
stroke sectioned by adroit
filament pitched inward or
outward depending on jaunt
that jig's sly the swagger
of the hidden source turns
on the pressure-baffled pi
of step and paces the foot
says pinch to danced tight
rhythms' log boogie woogie
and up tempo the dense off
the strata furl left lines
inventing the grasp solved
and the grasp parallel too

proof grew dizzy amending the parabola
proof dawned the amendment the longest
arc proof curved radiant grade testing
proof of indulged velocity to indulged
arc proof gained the form matched true

proof a width with a pin in it one per
proof a curve with a pin in it one per
arc proof nailed to the compass straps
proof emerges remnant magnetick lofted
arc proof piping the Ptolemaic to scat

proof parabola pressed Aesop in camera
proof the strata jargon of charting an
arc precedent to precedent hard upon a
proof first tongue convincible logic's
arc proof positive the Ptolemaic works

the measure of five the hand
to hand or the eyes' turn in
thought's measure or on foot
long tales of a traveller of
the journeyman his hands and

his eyes a wide span evasive
gaze picking the morning out
of thin air & know where the
sun waits in winter alien or
incongruous discussing roped

like Gulliver that loss with
a heap of stones the elusive
geometry of a wooden wall to
painted chair the shark that
as Noah-Ishmael he was twice

to elude his grotesque fable
certainties of what the worm
has secretly eaten confusion
the blunt tableau set like a
lament in a puzzle to answer

Beethoven Poulenc and a dictionary
wordwrack and sudden credit bathos
and butter permanent punctuation's
implicit whisper cocaine and roses
like the explicit axiom newspapers
theories this face reads strewn in
dimensions not words cheap glacial
the magic of an empty room and all
its fidelity to shadows and sounds
where pausing one goes crazy finds
his way again not so much on a new
path but the reaccomplished zeal a
properly nameless step that cannot
follow but that lifts this foot in
front of that foot to balance loss

Antares caught along a red wall
as straight as light can travel
the luminous portion emerges in
two sides of the glass or where
madness reluctantly out intuits
the exposure that light reforms
what the eye only realized form
as testimony form and frame the
instruments of reach surrounded

procession where extension begins
led out across what branches what
survives amazement past the stone
bridge and moored boats for these
shifting concessions of image and
the antiphonal the antiphonal raw

secure ungrudged root painted set
of edges the antiphonal makes the
neutral fullness a promise unkept
unspeakable equivalences securing
undiscoverable assertions choices
the solar the lunar & the stellar

elaborating the compromised taken
with the contradictory juxtaposed
intransigent suspect provoked and
inverted recognition's mirrorings
the exact turned verbal & nothing
for advance not even anticipation

the dry wheels grinding out
the cool pigments not green

not blue the age of clay in
ribbon brambled intricacies

selves' sap the marred sums
rigged spars of the dream's

oil and snow the strip link
scrawled on the obverse the

tall waves and verges terms
for eye and ear to register

beeswax and turpentine
Byzantine mesh argue a
Chinese strain forests
and decisions a vacant
light caught a sunrise
spoken moonset in this
reflection polished as
an idea without a used
context smoothed limit
primitive solace found
in water lit speech in
secrecy and song works
mouthread shape on the
tongue incognito hands
beeswax and turpentine

what heavy pearl what eye
fulfills the curious dark

something for everyone or
nothing for someone light

entrusted with place worn
smooth and dense as amber

bitten circumference wide
scatter solutionscape and

the abstract prejudice of
what prods to mystery and

what empties the upstream
transparent under the sun

glass limbo clear air not
the mind's round touching

with fugue in follow thru
reflection's waves lifted

resolve's subtle cast the
stressed floating in pair

ask Lazarus saved from
obscurity what ignored
might mean and glad as
he was to be taken out
of his white cave home
he'd say there's quite
no place like it yes I
may pong a bit but I'm
glad to be recalled in
time to be spoken to &
of Lazarus the slowest
pace a hand up on your
memory and what I know
now I will take my own
time in telling my own
time out of the shadow
of my past now you can
ask me anything but as
I will answer only out
of my own time you can
only wait hear and see

Medusa the forecast
accurate enough the
mind at bay renders
in stone and tattoo
informational light

the time it takes a
surfeit of fiddling
and fiddle scavenge
and calculate stone
accurate enough the

Medusa for forecast
large black letters
unowned literal and
fair torque's stone
to vibrating circle

purled dialogue adjunct
to the monologist's art
and the Pythagorean arc
its branches threaded a
descent standing on the
stump and this ascent a
measure of the step out
standing over the stump
perfection fits its eye
where the wind winds up

tender no
longer it
has taken
us in and
in good's
measure a
tender-to
and alone
no longer
we're the
caught in
the web a
grasp too
strong to
break too
tight and
tender no
longer it
holds you
and me in
measure's
time cuts
off short
breathing
fast from
tender to
tenderest
of ginger
ticking a
while hot
on tongue
lips move
the words
jump from
measure's
time to a
measure's
breathing

the sun shines abbreviating the
phenomenon known as sun rise at
the appointed hour high tide or
moon set what the papers record
so assiduously blander mementos
crayoned deep into metropolitan
canyons up one boulevard & down
another cruel and intimate this
negotiation or that evidence is
just another glamourous tyranny
booming the plight of a species
turning into a numbmare of lust
enchantment's occupational lurk
exploits the human universe one
at a time the moral advantage a
galaxy could offer fades in the
mists of premonition and craven
metabolism threat's bait effigy

a brief shrug puts a lengthy
stripe in the long phrase it
must be momentum or a shrewd

agreement based on time with
space a substitute for lucky
depths but allowing for heat

momentum is a sturdy running
time gone native doomed push
at gravity's moody pull much

to shrug about much to prove
if doubt's brief surge turns
to unanimous color and calms

to be or not to be from
an episode of composure
fragmented by reasoning

who stood where and why
who went where and when
reassembling the varied
sections took the whole
of a better idea into a
frontier of unsolved or
contrasting whims gyred

out of the next telling
blithe pseudo-classical
and city to city places

where who stood and why
who went there and when
further and further and
not without good reason
some stranded in shadow
others made the horizon
an episode of composure

odds or evens eye or ear

articulate sleep crossed

out receives the day's X

equals Y in applications

of desire and trust open

parentheses with slanted

wings tracing the rhythm

of flight in the opacity

of language gone outward

anything that moves

to reach that moves

anything into sight

to reach into moves

the simple souvenir

of a restive effort

who greeting whom
Goethe mehr Licht
quiet times & the
public sum greets
who greeting whom

clarity all's sum
else this hailing
of the quote from
Goethe mehr Licht
greets whom maybe

you caught around
the discrete word
in answer private
response survives
the call antiphon

mehr Licht Goethe
asked out loud is
it the darker sum
caught around the
eye or more Light

changes dimensioned one slice
of the crystal ones again and
again a pathetic tension heat
caught on my sleeve a dormant
Aetna distraction's attentive
blooms in snow changes flaked
and humbled the turn past the
focus a weathered edge fixing
the continuity split quadrant
no simple hole but a carboned
knot whose core is remembered
silence tooth's recall enough
penetrated facets one and one
again and again raw mirage in
the cutter's eye noble scorch

lift light minus the eye
lifts light minus this I
pressure stretched tight
across tight against the
site regime situate goad
poised taut as the glare
jagged patch on the eyed
hard white as pain bread
turned inside out rhymes
houri and hours insomnia
navigates this periphery
flare by flare frictions
to transparency oracular
count in a broken circle

the instant minute fingers
change just to look like a
look at or what would have
worked out or worked up to
look that way an instant a
here and now resolved warm
almost led out of the blue
the endless island creases
island arrow twists in the
space it projects feigning
883 miles to the pole webs
to untangle plight's blurs
in the so called head find
respite in the instant day
to day squeezes from truth
the wedge placed best thin
as a scalpel alerts recall
time slides under the most
explicit boxed inside this
ply after ply of if before
I particularized for place
time slides under the most
implicit coaxed aside this
ply under ply of if before
I particularized for scale

like looking for a navel in a
haystack cold sorties cold in
control cross rose and violet
and influence sureness factor
out color and you have thrown
a frame oiled the hollow with
a comfortable distance curfew
against the pane a figure and
and its weight reserve papers
the sky to the north sighting
the vernacular cold rising in
short columns of smoke static
gnawing at the patterns of an
impenetrable conversation far
and yes or no capsulize these
wavelengths damaged terms are
humbling the circular idiom a
reciprocal validity talks the
attention the metered road on
the varied bands is stuck tip
in the plus hulled in the red
measure spiral the green mons
of muscle and vast haze tiers
thin and wild where the grass
burns argued the translations
unused flashbacks stored with
the drones soft lattice where
the numbers can run thirty to
this wavelength preempts pace
stiff time peels the ray wire

what the eye picks out of the metaphysical
distance it has already built, torn down &
built up again USE is not this transparent
change but what is built and abandoned set
against itself alone barely tolerant of an
horizonhorizonhorizonhorizonhorizonhorizon

vapor bush and strings bateau forte
smoked dye all a cloth rainbow keys
rinsed in sunlight clockwarp just a
blade's share left in the ivy right
in the loosestrife how to find fast
the water's edge pearl in monotones
lampcough and gapside the patchwork
pedal play and a few half notes too
stairs and a few whole notes batter
banjo scales not knots fishing in a
toothache plumblot for kitchen dial
the weather brogues changing at sea
iron scales and an ear bucket oiled
boats between the cloudsails mizzen
to testament and augmented languors

a kerf then a crescent kerf
zero to zero and back again

broken spiral by addition a
nest of gems in the gravity

azimuths oboes and runes so
tense the unacknowledged so

move then numbers to shapes
and the object in mind word

relaxed in homonymy and the
coincident kept open always

mouth to mouths utters what
what to say the prophecy is

this awkwardness reduced to
touch however briefly first

the lost family of scatter cabal
thought under disorder and music
filling the crumpled space owned
by another taught under disorder
to make a path through judgement
the music the piles of paper the
knocking at the door the silence
of the one another small breaths
before bread to embarass the one
or two crabbed beats of unspoken
dreams eye to eye what was wrong
never to find its words the wall
harvesting the dust and echoes a
comfort was the intruder knowing
whatever made would not stay not
a word not hungers just disorder

the dazzling flaw seen from the
inside an alternative hive adds
vogue hybrids to vague settings

ubiquitous & complicated a body
in motion its unfinished shadow
the way of a larger claim light

has on the transparent and most
eccentric or circuitous impulse
hand on hip hip extended repeat

the conjunction of the muscular
and the conceptualized kin both
cut up and frayed as ferns cool

intelligence cool flesh defiled
and mythic the preference turns
a chalkmark a hairline a timing

always flexible and always idle
the unfinished spectrum handled
like the well-timed distraction

but fidelity creates its own
necessity the object the one
place the lines cross a numb
carapace fidelity everything
adjusted the pygmy share and
a glance between the scratch
and the split remnant search
is the fire too wide an idea
shelved with deaf courtesy a
rhythm as wide in the pathos
the obedient center bonds it
too hard to hold too long it
makes its stray and negative
amendations shut or dimmed a
captive of fidelity's rigors

Italian has always
the operatic heart
poems oaths & song

Americani or maybe
merd di cani Dante
& Boccaccio caught

fast on the tongue
say old poison the
strongest familiar

as ink wine & gold
the red days burnt
umber hoofbeats in

the bonfire temper
mistrust & cryptic
melancholy origins

backed into the odors of a
metropolitan hillside dead
leaves plunge into blasted
clouds falsetto taxis come
bringing the prurient some
small scandals hoary scars
and a few brittle shouts a
sense of the unanimous has
abandoned the weather gone
away with the taxis backed
out along the joyless rain
making its way up the hill
rote catastrophes crossing
the manicured lawns shrill
hoaxes intoned in C# minor

spruce as the zodiac prompted by
theology or spruce as the zodiac
corrected by theology Herr Dürer

I should say Mr Dürer or nothing
at all (O bone-dry apostle) aqua
alta dispatched from shot towers

forget the medieval now it's all
speed mathematicks and em spaces
spelled out in quandaries indext

with unique and cynical mappings
what complicates the uncanny the
critical the next said using the

roof to build the walls startled
ground dug in and planted method
to extend the present in what is

found there in the past the slip
of the seed & the pursuit of the
scythe was the private wasted on

what is factored out an offering
book and board plank and shelter
the white page and its hard ears

allegro blind–touched horizons
of feathers wool and silk spot
the pairs of miracles feathers
wool and lint hot black yellow
orange and blue debt's bunting
suspended from a pallid signal
debt's sleep fixed by a pulsed
signal the small thousand made
the phrase valvecraft the cold
blanket now and I now or I now
and I or now so intent on song
or where the corner of the eye
puts a foundry around the dome
of the heart so intent on song

exposed to the lacelight of
the sun grinding ground wet
ground dry colors solace so
solicited where it begins X
where the light ends or Y &
where the shadow begins and
the light begins again face
what the light builds twice
rough carbon use of the sky

one and one and one are three
and one is seven the arm fast
in the dark a prompting touch
you one you say you saw touch
hands over hands dizzy comets
winter-dark the aloof spirals
fat stars milk brass and snow

a pattern within the numbered
simplicity dances in the fire
assay the bright eye makes in
the darkness printed within a
spectrum transition's quantum
line for lines lines to lines
step for steps jumps to color

extract scars or knot pursuit
opens in the living judgement
self less intervals of flight
poise a pyramid of deflection
its form scraped from silence
tools exposed in the syllable
sunlight draping the mountain

your words
gripped in
stammering

forked air
anvil plow
in the gap

floods the
paradox of
oneness in

discordant
cunning it
points the

tongue and
enclave an
outsider's

stark mute
abrasion a
hub of the

calm blind
gripped in
time twice

the sparks
words work
in turning

gripped in
stammering
your words

greased before the count chagrin
pinned to the foot hurried music
prized whores broken drumrolls a
shriven carnival Ottoman Turk in
Cyprus Crete and the Levant cold
tongue hot lips counterfeit torn
from the fragmentary forfeit and
derelict scarce a likeness aloof
its Byzantine proportions gnawed
to the shine continuum's aphasia

circumscribe the enthusiastic
lament reliant drone first in
factitious tragedy shouts and
props the anxious prodigal by
his oracle for a specimen odd
of thought's boon enchantment
extinction of the contestable
extract this chronic velocity
stepping through that minimum
to Alcibiades on election day
mean staring and sober storms
just the interim of hyperbole
the future a perfume tucked a
long while into a subjunctive
non-sequitur priapic and calm

static answers static to
paraphrase what discards
and dissolves to protect
affinities never located
what homage restructures
and what wraps the logos
in snarls of postulation
precise bearing restored
not disclosed obdurate a
mortal burr and accuracy
admired by a distinctive
sense of continuity heat
cut with idleness making
amends for melancholy or
perfecting the unmeasure

as simultaneous and
dissolving as drops
to torture as drops
to instant as drops
to substance chains
taken along singing
resolution the link
pronounced the coin
as drops dissolving
in drops of instant
details singing out
well expressionless
as torpid spectacle
as graced in frenzy
as proven in frenzy

for solitude a primordial mirage
globes and somber arcades neoned
dioramas word for word rue de 12
o'clock echo the lacquered laugh

of centi genti a latch on the un
sayable the unforgettable plan a
skull blue burning north measure
allure for bees in the catalogue

a gratitude under the azure hide
of centi genti red grass meadows
the answers misspoken the or the
of centi genti no until no palms

remembered one hand to the shape
is either a mystery or a lie two
voices thickened in moonlight no
hand raised to dim the glare won

slow revolve slow revolve slow
revolve in the chambered cleft
lynx blunt mud post scan frets
spooled in the drum gather aim
and tool barrel hewn out of it
fluted stock mixed woods resin
overtoned then lowered slowing
opened nod sluice of wool noon
hot throats a cone prods drops
stones sop in the baffled viol

the root intervals beyond explanation
correspondence the single arrangement
new to life though ancient as methods
and categories of thought the elegant
washing of the roar the completed ray
of blood and air trapped in the means
fleeing the retrieval-taut reflection

high as the wind changes the reach
sanctions spiral over the faces of
apprehended change more than times
of upheaval twisted in the drift a
clamorous uncertainty on the skids
no more than that but more than it
seems nickelodeon rhetoric barking
at a raw nerve evaporated song its
sand and leaves in the throat hold
the flash glacier in the eye again

we have seen what you mean and can't
a good word but a leprous honesty in
the reply (question) how else to put
it (question) how much do you know a
tall bearded man in a white shirt or
how much do you want to know (I only
ask because of the way in which I've
chosen to dress today) (as question)
(or what the question implies) tints
(hints) or turpitude a short bearded
man in a red shirt was also seen his
reply was a further question implied
were (question) should and something
ominous a covenant with memory and a
good eye for color though faulted (a
further question) by the way a quick
shadow fell across the short bearded
man in the red (question) shirt seen
where the man in white is thought to
have been seen misunderstandings red
in the wrong light white in shadow a
beard (question) or beards (how much
does the error or confusion imply is
it white in shadow now or was it red
reply to the shadow or colors reply)

habitation has its own potencies
expecting nothing forfeit at the
end of the road-- instinct and a
dictionary einfach one phase the
fifth refuge for pattern's count

out of the hectic vernacular the
solemn but unsophisticated tales
conspiratorial the wings a large
W mimic-dulled creak in the gold
leaf refused the pattern's count

or severed like a conjugation of
discoveries R steps encephalic a
subversion of portents reforming
the pattern's contes impedimenta
fifth refuge for pattern's count

provident decem worked within
the unmade exists in the open
one way under the moon spared
one way under the stars match
one way under the sun another
at the edge of the desk nexus
of optical eccentricities and
a balcony of syllables arches
and piers safe as time within
sight the ornament of eclipse

Of this edition, 26 have been lettered A through Z
and signed by the author.